My
Uninvited
GUEST

Stephanie M. Dorsch

ISBN: 978-1-4834-4245-7 (sc)
ISBN: 978-1-4834-4246-4 (e)

Lulu Publishing Services rev. date: 11/26/2015

Contents

Chapter One

||||||||||||||||||||||||||||||||||||||||||||||||||||||||||||||||||||||||||||||||||||||||||||||||||||||||

STEPHANIE'S STORY

I grew up in Summerhill, Pennsylvania which in 1950 had a population of 1000 people. I never realized that the population was that large. When I was ten we had a monumental change in our family. We moved into our new home: it had been a two-story, four-car garage on my paternal grandparents' property. Through the years my parents updated and added on to the home. It provided shelter and hospitality to anyone who entered. The family had use of the home for more than sixty years.

Growing up in Summerhill was a wonderful adventure. But, of course I could not get away with anything. I am the oldest of four children. My dad kept me on a short leash. Walking home with him one day he said "I want you to remember that when you meet someone you are to say hello", because saying hello is being polite and easier to do than turning your head.

Sunday was always a special day. It was the day dad took us for a ride in the car. We usually went to Altoona, Pennsylvania to visit relatives. As a three-year-old the excitement of going to visit cousins with my parents was appealing. The cousins represented a whole new world to me. Their bedroom was located in the attic of their home. I always looked forward to exploring this magical room, strewn with women's unmentionables, make up and costume jewelry. My cousin wasn't interested in these wonders, since she saw her older sisters getting

1

dressed every day. But it turned out it was going to be a long time before I went to the attic room again.

On our way to Altoona my mother, hearing a noise in the back of the car, saw the door was opened, but didn't see me. I had fallen out. She grabbed my brother, who was on his way to follow me. In those days cars didn't have the safety features they now have. Stopping the car dad gathered me up and took me to the hospital where I stayed about a week with a skull fracture. Some think this was the beginning of my Parkinson's.

As a young girl I didn't need to find friends as there were plenty in my town. Our school was a one-story brick building. There were five girls and twelve boys in the class. For a while the room that housed the second and third grade was empty because there was no teacher. Later, a young, new teacher was hired and we were so happy to have her and were charmed by her. We wanted to have some sort of club and asked her for recommendations. After much discussion we agreed to join the Girl Scouts. It was a good idea and the start of the first Girl Scout Troop in Summerhill. Today, there is a Girl Scout Camp located in the nearby woods above Summerhill and is called Camp Conshatawba.

When our school system was absorbed by a larger local system, both the Girl Scout Troop and the close knit group of girls was broken up. All the children were bused to another school. It was a learning experience I didn't much like because we were pitted against each other to be better than the other. Not knowing the other children created dissension.

Looking back, when winter came it didn't fool around. Even though it was a small town we were not hindered by the snow, nor did we see cars slipping and sliding on the road. When the big white fluffy flakes would fall my favorite place was the dining room window. It was a large picture window. I could drape myself on the inside of the window and watch the snow fall. I was in the dining room a lot because my job was to set the table. The reason there weren't any stranded car or drivers spinning their wheels was that the road winding through our town was a state-maintained road. When the big snow plows came from their barracks they were fully loaded for any type of weather problems. The trucks always left a plowed road, a clean, white road. From my window it looked warm and inviting but I knew the opposite was true. It was cold and windy outside with the snow drifting across the road.

Because of my age I was on the tail end of the snow sledding time. In earlier times people made large wooden sleds and they were called toboggans. Mother had my "black watch" wool pants lined with flannel material and they were the warmest pants.

Dad came home about 4:30 pm and was always in a rush. During dinner I would watch the snow accumulation. I could do this easily as my chair faced the window, so I knew when dinner was over how deep the snow was. If I played it right I could get dad to get my sled out of the garage. It was a humorous situation for the family because, as soon as the snow began to fall I would need to get the sled out.

Winter turned into spring and I found myself baby- sitting my new born brother. He was fun to be around and I spent many hours dressing him in costumes. Many days I missed lunch with the family because it was my brother's bed time and I was putting him to bed.

The summer of my 16th birthday two events happened: first, I talked my godfather into bringing electricity into and wiring the one room cabin that was located on our property in the country. We would spend all our leisure time there. The cabin was partially built from an earlier cabin on the property and we moved it and enlarged it. Not having told dad, he was naturally unhappy with this venture. He would not give us the money to finish the job. Dad didn't like to charge anything. The following year he finished the job. We had to wait till we could afford to pay for it.

The second event was the building of our pool. It was built of concrete blocks and pond water fed, but what made it really nice was the two electric lights that lite the night.

The water was green-looking and was like ice but we didn't care, any excuse to get into the pool was acceptable. We would go swimming whenever we could. It was grand. In the mountains of Pennsylvania the water was cold, even in the summer.

One of my cousins came to visit and she was so excited, as she was going to Mount Aloysius in the fall for her freshman year of college. She told me her mother, having been to the hairdresser, related this to her when she got home. She said that the Academy was there, too. Later I told my dad about going to the Mount to finish high school but he said no. His mother found out about this and told him I should go. My grandmother had gone to boarding school when she was my age and felt it would be good for me.

A whole new world opened to me. I had looked forward to my once-a-month routine of going next door to my grandparents' house where I would sit in my grandfather's rocking chair and would read *Life, Look,* and *Vogue* magazines. When I went to the Mount I wandered into the periodical room. There I found a continuation of what I had done at home. I read the magazines, but a new wrinkle entered the picture: I found the large newspapers. With *The New York Times, The Washington Post, The Wall Street Journal,* and *The Philadelphia Enquirer,* the world was opening up and the principles I developed at the Mount have stayed with me.

After I married and moved south I had to learn new social skills in this new world that was so different. My husband traveled, leaving me to take care of the home and children. Having four children in twelve years I found it hard to cope. Not having family nearby to help or rely on made it even harder. I was used to being next door to my paternal grandmother and the aunts. My mother's family lived a few blocks away and I missed them terribly.

Everything had to be planned so that I could be with the children at school activities, keep the house clean and have meals ready. I found it hard to communicate over the phone and came to hate discussing anything on the phone. I found I had to take hold of the situations and become more outgoing and assertive, but my insecurities were many, especially after I was diagnosed with Parkinson's. I kept all this to myself.

When I learned that I had Parkinson's I never imagined it could be something so unusual and that I didn't just have a cold which I would eventually get over. I found that I had something known as a designer disease, which is a disease that is not common or well understood. The forms of PD are many and varied and affect everyone differently. A doctor can't tell you that first you will do this and then you will do that. For the first ten years I went to the doctor every month and my medications stayed the same.

The medications controlled my shaking very well, and at one point the doctor said it was as if the disease was arrested.

Before I was 50 I liked to paint and refinish furniture. I also liked to make clothing for the girls and things for the house. Trying to think back can be difficult, but I remember that I always liked to make things. I always wanted to be a part of the community, I liked volunteering and going to plays. I still do, but now it has become too complicated for me to go.

Since I was spending so much time at home with the children and with the Parkinson's I had to find some activity that I could do at home to stay active. My favorite activity at that time was learning to sew. The first job I did was making drapes for my large window in the family room. I had read that I should take my window measurements with me to the fabric store. The clerk waiting on me was measuring out so much material. I didn't say anything but I thought she had over-sold me on the yardage. I went home and began to cut the pattern out. I could not understand why I had so much material left over. Going back to the store, to see if I could find out what I did wrong, I found the material had a pattern and I had not allowed for the repeat. That is why the clerk gave me more material.

The next sewing project was making clothes and I liked the challenge of creating something from tearing out a garment and remaking it.

One day I decided to remove the paint from the wood work in a small powder room. Even though the window was open, the odor—the stench—was caustic. Today I still remember the smell and wonder if this was the cause of my PD. The house had originally been painted with lead paint.

My husband suggested we take a real estate course, thinking that might help me and allow me to get out with people. I had not been to school for many years and was not used to the banter that goes on and soon found I did not have good study habits. So I tried to develop them by disciplining myself. Every morning after taking the girls to school, I would straighten the house and then go into the same room, at the same time of day, every day and study from 9am until 11am. By doing this, I surprised myself by passing the tests and earning my broker's license. I then worked real estate for a few years. I was just starting to make inroads with selling when I was diagnosed with Parkinson's.

My husband gets agitated with me because I don't react like a person without PD. It is so silly that I have to giggle. My situation is so final, I have no recourse. We can't always have everything and this put the end to some of the things I considered important. With my being alone and not having companionship at home, I missed my extended family.

Fortunately with my Parkinson's not advancing, I was able to become involved with the Garden Club which gave me the opportunity to become a Flower Show Judge, an activity I dearly love. This activity helped me to overcome my shyness, but I still have problems. When I think all that I have accomplished I am amazed at myself because I find I get so tongue tied. As I have never talked about this before it amazes me. I made the decision when I started to write this story that I would be frank and truthful.

The day came when I received a letter from the state of North Carolina telling me I was not to do any driving over 45 miles an hour. That was devastating to me. It cut me off from shopping, meeting friends, visiting family and going to the movies. I had always taken myself when I wanted to do something. Now I had to call friend to ask if they could take me. Not being used to this made it hard for me to do. Parkinson's put up more barriers for me.

When I go shopping I like to look around at things to see what is available. Now I find friends don't want to just wait and so I am pressured to just get what I said I wanted, and then go home. My world is getting smaller.

Now I find I can't remember what happened. I try to keep a daily run-down of my activities so I can recall what I have done. This causes me to be stressed while I cope with my uninvited guest. It's an "I'll be damned no matter what" sort of situation.

I hear comments like, "Stephanie always has a smile on her face." I do this deliberately because a Parkinson's face is a flat stare, a strained look. No one wants to be around a stone face. For these reasons I am able to get out among people and being around others is helpful. It also helps me to cope with the everyday trials I carry within myself. If I hurt, or my foot, leg or toes hurt, how do they carry me? These are the marks of a warrior. I am a warrior. I will not stop, but press on!

Chapter Two

||||||||||||||||||||||||||||||||||||||||||||||||||||||||||||||||||||||||||||||||||||||||||||||||||||||||||

WHAT IS PARKINSON'S DISEASE?

Parkinson's disease (PD) is a progressive neurological disorder that destroys the individual's motor control—the ability to control their muscles and movements—and robs them of their independence. It is more common in people over 60, but the number of people diagnosed at a younger age is increasing.

PD often begins with a slight tremor and difficulty initiating voluntary movements and progresses throughout life with a range of distressing symptoms. It becomes increasingly disabling, making daily activities such as bathing or dressing difficult or impossible. It slowly advances to difficulty dealing with pain, depression, loss of balance, gastrointestinal problems, memory loss, mood swings, loss of sleep, swallowing, and involuntary movements. As the disease progresses, some people may need to use a wheelchair or may even become bedridden. Dementia may occur in some people.

The primary symptoms are:

1. Tremor – Shaking of a limb or the whole body. This is the most recognized symptom of PD. Not everyone has tremors.

2. Rigidity – Stiffness or inflexibility of the limbs or joints. It often begins in the neck and legs. It affects most people and many feel pain or stiffness.
3. Bradykinesia – Slowness of movement or absence of movement. Over a period of time a slow shuffling walk and stooped posture may develop.
4. Postural Instability – Impaired balance and coordination. A person may have a stooped posture. They may develop a forward or backward lean and the tendency to fall increases with the possibility of injuries. With a backward lean, there is a tendency to step backwards.

PD is caused by the degeneration of a small part of the brain called the *substantia nigra*. As brain cells in the *substantia nigra* die, the brain becomes deprived of the chemical, dopamine. Dopamine enables brain cells involved in movement control to communicate, and reduced levels lead to the symptoms of PD. According to the National Parkinson's Foundation, 60% to 80% of dopamine producing cells are lost before the motor symptoms of PD appear. Parkinson's a formidable opponent. It affects over one million Americans, and at present there is no cure. Every nine minutes someone is diagnosed with Parkinson's. That is 60,000 people a year. Scientists believe that one day a cure will be found. It is not a question of if, but when. Throughout the world, scientists are dedicated to unraveling the mystery of what causes the disease, but more clinical research is needed to find solutions to this life draining disease. That is why there is so much effort to get funding for research.

I had the DBS operation (two implants) on June 26, 2003. To give you more information about the brain surgery (DBS) that I had, here is some information from an article by Medtronic, "Living with DBS Therapy," that I found on the internet.

"Deep Brain Stimulation (DBS) is a surgical procedure used to treat a variety of disabling neurological symptoms—most commonly the debilitating symptoms of PD, such as tremors, rigidity, stiffness, slowed movement, and walking problems. DBS surgery does not damage healthy brain tissue by destroying nerve cells. Instead the procedure blocks electrical signals from targeted areas in the brain. At present the procedure is used only for patients whose symptoms can't be adequately controlled with medications.

A surgically implanted battery operated medical device called a neurostimulator, similar to a heart pacemaker and about the size of a stopwatch, delivers electrical stimulation to targeted areas of the brain that control movement, thereby blocking the abnormal nerve signals that cause tremors and 22 other PD symptoms. Before the surgery a neurosurgeon uses magnetic resonance imaging (MRI) or computer tomography (CT) scanning to identify and locate the exact target within the brain where electrical nerve signals generate the PD symptoms. Surgeons may use microelectrode recordings, which involves placing a small wire that monitors the activity of nerve cells in the target area, to more specifically identify the precise target that will be stimulated."

Generally the targets are the thalamus, sub thalamic nucleus, and Globus Pallid. Once the implants are in place, electrical impulses are sent from the neurostimulator, long extension wires, into the implants. These impulses interfere with and block the electrical signals that cause the PD symptoms.

How do I know if I am a good candidate for the surgery I asked myself? As I realized what the criteria were, I found that I had every one of them. I was very excited to be eligible for the operation.

Here are some of the criteria:

- You have had PD symptoms for at least five years.
- You have "on/off" fluctuations" with or without dyskinesia.
- You continue to have a good response to PD medications, especially carbidopa/levodopa although the duration of response may be insufficient.
- You have tried different combinations of levodopa/carbidopa and pain agonists under the supervision of a movement disorders neurologist.

- You have tried other PD medications such as entacapone, tolcapone, selegiline, or amanadine without beneficial results.
- You have PD symptoms that interfere with daily activities.

What is the prognosis? Although most patients still need to take medications after undergoing DBS surgery, many patients may experience a considerable reduction of their PD symptoms and are able to greatly reduce their medications. The amount of reduction varies from patient to patient but can be considerably reduced in most patients. The reduction in the dose of medication leads to a significant improvement in side effects such as dyskinesia (involuntary movements caused by long term use of levodopa).

There is a 1% to 3% chance of infection, stroke, cranial bleeding, or other complications associated with anesthesia, per side that is done. These risks must be discussed with your neurologist prior to the operation.

I truly believe I would not be alive had I not had the DBS. It has given me 20 years of good living.

> Medtronic, the manufacturer, of the Deep Brain Stimulator for Parkinson's can be found at www. medtronicdbs.com

Chapter Three

||||||||||||||||||||||||||||||||||||||||||||||||||||||||||||||||||||||||||||||||||||||||||||||||||||||||||||||||||||||||||||

OUR PARKINSON'S COMMUNITY

In 2009, The National Parkinson's Foundation (NPF), launched an unprecedented research collaboration known as the Quality Improvement Initiative (QII), which was part of the Parkinson's Outcome Project. It is the largest clinical study of Parkinson's disease (PD) ever conducted and the first with the primary goal of identifying and explaining factors that result in longer, and more active people with PD.

The study encompasses 20 leading centers for treating Parkinson's, all part of NPF's Center of Excellence network. By studying the "best of the best," the NPF plans to delve into key differences in treatment and outcomes because every person with PD deserves "best practice" care, no matter where they are treated. The result is the largest pool of Parkinson's data ever collected, from 5,500 patients in four countries. If you have Parkinson's there is someone like you participating in the study, some thriving and others doing less well. The goal is to determine what makes the difference.

Unlike prior studies, this initiative encompasses the entire spectrum of physical and mental conditions. When we study how disease affect individuals, we talk about your "Health Status" and much of this report concerns the Health Status of people in the study. Health status is important because it encompasses much more than just the disease.

The goal of a physician is not to just help you function better, but to help you feel better. There is a difference between function and feeling. How people with Parkinson's feel—their mood and depression—is a critical factor with a tangible impact on overall health. The study also identified some of the steps, that as doctors, and you as patients, can make. These opportunities for all to improve health are the highlight of this inaugural report.

It is hoped that the next major breakthrough in Parkinson's disease will be a treatment that slows down the biological progression. When this is achieved, optimizing care will be even more important; though symptoms may be reduced, they will have to be addressed over a longer life expectancy. Working together to prevent falls, treating depression, and addressing other factors that can speed the deterioration of one's health will improve one's quality of life. As breakthroughs are achieved, care will become more personalized, so that the best therapies are applied to your particular situation. In short, the goal is not only to optimize today's care, but to help guide tomorrow's.

Our gratitude goes out to the patients, caregivers, researchers and all others who participate in helping to fill in the gaps in our understanding of this disease.

The First World Parkinson's Day

The following information is listed to highlight the efforts that have been made to get the public and government to recognize the impact PD has on the patients and their care givers. This effort has been going on for many years and at all levels of government:

April 11, 1997 was celebrated as the First World Parkinson's Disease Day initiated by the World Health Organization and the European Parkinson's Disease Association. The United States Disease Association, the American Parkinson's Disease Association, the National Parkinson's Foundation, the United Parkinson's Foundation and the Parkinson's Foundation all participated in this project.

April 9, 1997 bill 1260 was introduced to Congress, simultaneously in both houses, by Representative Fred Upton and Senator John McCain respectively. The house had 111 co- sponsors while the senate had 37.

April 23, 1997 Muhammad Ali testified before the House Appropriations Committee in support of the Morris K. Udahl Research and Education Act bill. Senator Udahl of Oregon developed PD while in congress. His condition was visible.

April 24, 1997 the governor of North Carolina, James B. Hunt, issued a proclamation recognizing April as Parkinson's Awareness Month.

January 14, 2015 Rep. Michael Burgess (R-TX) and Chris Van Hollen (D-MD) co-sponsored bill HR 292, entitled "The Advancing Research for Neurological disease Ac of 2015." This bill has not been passed as yet.

July 10, 2015, HR 6 was passed by the U. S. House of Representatives, entitled "The 21 Century Cares Act" provides for the development of new treatments for Parkinson's and other diseases, and for developing Data Collection Systems. This is considered an important milestone for a historic piece of legislation. It includes one of PAN's top policy priorities, the advancing of research for Neurological Parkinson's disease. It also invests in critical medical research at the National Institute of Health and the Food and Drug Administration and encourages patient-focused drug development.

Mind over Matter

I wrote this article a while ago and it was published in a book entitle "Eat Well, Stay Well with Parkinson's Disease" written by Kathrynne Holden published in 1998. I recently reread it and find that it is still timely.

"Parkinson's Disease has given me a very complicated puzzle to work with each day. Yes, exercise is an important key. Recently I was preoccupied with a concern, so I went to my garden to weed. As I was walking back into the house I realized that I felt, better mentally and physically. The power of our mind can improve things for us by not letting negative acts or opinions influence us. I am going to the YMCA three times a week and exercising on a Nautilus machine for an hour. Then I walk on the treadmill for 30 minutes and I feel good that I am able to do this and stay in shape. It made me feel good that I was able to do this and stay in shape. I will celebrate my 57th birthday in 1995 and my 8th with My Un-Invited Guest."

This year, 2015, I will celebrate my 76th birthday and I will have had Parkinson's for 28 years.

Chapter four

||||||||||||||||||||||||||||||||||||||||||||||||||||||||||||||||||||||||||||||||||||||||||||||||||||||

NON-MOTOR SYMPTOMS and AUTONOMIC DYSFUNCTION

Parkinson's disease is diagnosed on the basis of motor symptoms which include slowness of movement, tremors, rigidity and difficulty with walking and balance. It is now known that non-motor symptoms are important and might start before motor symptoms.

Parkinson's disease is not diagnosed by a test. It is diagnosed by looking at a patient's medical records and an examination of the patient. Screening for non-motor symptoms may aid accurate diagnosis. It is estimated that Parkinson's disease shows itself about 6 years after it begins. Studies have shown that PD can effect serotonin levels, which are associated with depression. Knowledge is freeing and research is the answer. Depression may have the greatest impact on health status. Almost twice that of motor symptoms.

I think that a decreased sense of smell was the first symptom I noticed I had lost. I could no longer smell what I was making or cooking. Constipation, bladder problems, sexual problems, excessive saliva, weight loss, vision and dental problems, fatigue, loss of energy, cognitive issues, depression and anxiety, skin problems, fear, memory difficulties, slowed thinking, confusion and in some cases, dementia, medication side effects, such as impulsive behaviors, are all common problems in PD.

When I get up at night to urinate it amazes me how many times I need to get up.

Balance has been a problem for me from day one. It impacts on very thing I do. My feet don't want to move when I am ready to move. I have slowed so much.

I find that if I get to bed about 10:30 I will go right to sleep. However, about 2 or 3 am I get awake and stay awake until about 4 am. I also found that I am having severe night sweats. They start in my stomach area and my neck and finally my hair will be sopping wet. I must get out of bed to change my clothes. It is a chore to get out of bed and change clothes and crawl back into bed. My time clock is all messed up. I don't want to go to sleep in the evening.

My mind is too full of thoughts. I want to do my house work in the evenings instead of the day time when I am able to walk more easily. It seems as if I have a stop on my moving during the day and then I find I am able to move better in the evenings. My nights are filled with things that put me off sleeping.

The non-motor symptoms like sleep and thinking skills, energy levels and emotional well-being have been recognized as important and need to be observed along with changes a person experiences with the body's motors skills. One area that training is helpful, is thinking. This training, known as Cognitive Training, refers to the process of thinking. This training attempts to improve the speed of thinking and the ability to remember and express words. Many PD patients have this problem and don't recognize that it is a problem. Cognitive training has shown improvement in everyday activities such as driving. Drivers are more alert. The primary cause of memory and thinking problems is biological, meaning these problems are due to changes in the structure and chemistry of the brain. These same changes are experienced by PD patients. Most PD patients who show clinical signs of dementia will on autopsy show these changes in the brain.

Autonomic Dysfunction

Two thirds of PD patients have signs and symptoms of autonomic dysfunctions (AD) which may have substantially changed their quality of life. AD controls a number of functions in the body involving the cardiovascular system: blood pressure, heart rate, sexual arousal, and thermo-regulation, and even plays a role in more active functions like swallowing.

Cardiovascular changes and orthostatic hypotension are also common in PD patients and are significant risk factors for falls, mobility, and mortality. Early identification of risk factors, careful diagnosis, and the treatment of vascular disease may help reduce the health outcomes related to the severity of autonomic dysfunctions. Dizziness and freezing may occur when there is a drop in blood pressure.

If you are experiencing orthostatic hypotension talk with your doctor.

Avoid crossing your legs while sitting and sit up and stand up slowly so you don't fall as a result of over-balancing.

Swallowing dysfunctions pose a significant health hazard. I have been bothered with what feels like a knot in my throat. At times I cough because I want to keep my throat open. I cough and the problem stays the same. It doesn't go away. It is not any pleasure to have a problem like this.

I also suffer from a bleeding nose. After seeing a specialist I found that putting moisture (nose drops/spray) in my nose morning and night helps keep my nose moist and reduces the bleeding. The same applies to my eyes. I need to use eye drops. I also have to keep my mouth damp since I have a dry mouth. I drink a lot of water. When I take a swallow of water I swish it around in my mouth and my gums feel so much better.

Freezing is a serious problem that I have. It is not a pleasure to have a problem like this and it makes it very hard to walk. Freezing is a common problem and freezing issues are frustrating and increase the risk of falling because you never know when you are going to freeze. It just happens!

Night sweats and urinary problems are other problems that bother me. Many nights I get awake and my hair is sopping wet. It is not fun, but I am most distressed that I can't hold my water. When I have the urge to go I must hurry to relieve myself or I will wet myself. I wear a pad to help protect myself from having an accident. The longer a person lives with PD, their symptoms will become more difficult to handle.

Information, education, and a better understanding of autonomic dysfunctions will help a person to better manage their non-motor symptoms. Knowing is better.

Chapter five

MY UNINVITED GUEST

This story is about my Uninvited Guest, Parkinson's disease, also known as PD. I am not sure how I came up with this expression. To some it might be explained easily, but it is not a term of endearment. It is a strong term of disgust and I do not want it. I hate it. It has made my life unbearable and I have given up doing many things I enjoyed because of it.

Parkinson's disease (PD) is an uncharted frontier and at times it can be very scary. I do not know what to expect. PD affects everyone differently and it is considered a designer disease.

PD is called a designer disease because the symptoms vary with individuals.

Some mornings when I wake and try to get up, I can't. I must grip the mattress and pull myself up and out of bed. And sometimes when I get up I feel like I am going to fall backwards. I try to make sure I am holding securely onto something or sitting down. These problems don't happen every day, but now they are happening more often. Now I must plan ahead and be prepared for the unexpected. I don't just get up and walk. I am scared of the unknown.

When I wake I find the first digits on my hands are swollen and numb and at times my feet feel like they are swollen. When I move the numbness goes away. My feet are changing. I find the left foot has a bunion on it making it hard to walk.

Every morning when the flowers are in bloom I like to walk in my garden and look at the flowers. I am constantly surprised at the way nature works and how the opening of a flower can happen. When I go out to get the paper I wear my fisherman's boots and a rubber raincoat because I realize that I might fall. If I should, these items help to cushion my fall. My balance is so fragile that I often do. I also use my walker and a cane to help prevent my falling. The walker helps me to get about in the yard. If I see a flower further in the garden than I can reach, I use the cane to assist my going further into the garden to see the flower up close.

On one occasion I fell in my yard and I bruised myself badly on my left breast. I had been walking around my yard and saw some loose bricks that I thought I could stack. Leaning forward I started to fall. I tried to stabilize myself by reaching for a small bush but I missed grabbing on to the bush and I was dazed from the fall. It was not a fall of heights but it was devastating to me. My breast was black and blue for six months and to this day I still have a few black spots. I am amazed that with my many falls I have not seriously hurt myself.

I was concerned that the fall might have damaged my DBS batteries since the bruises were so close to the location of the batteries. A few weeks earlier I had surgery to replace the batteries. A check-up proved the bruises were close, but had not caused any problems.

I fall so often that the skin on my knees is always broken or bleeding. In order to give some protection, I bought a pair of soccer knee pads which I wear. They work very well in providing the extra cushioning and they fit under slacks and dresses. The idea of wearing knee pads came to me as I watched my young daughter wear them to play soccer.

My most spectacular fall was in my kitchen, while trying to turn around I over balanced myself then fell in to the double ovens. I shattered. The glass on the bottom oven door. It was a miracle I was not hurt. I had another fall which precede this fall about 26 years earlier. While leaving a friends kitchen I balanced myself while leaving a friend's kitchen through her garage. I was carrying a glass platter, which I was concerned about breaking. I slipped and fell down two steps, hurting my back on the treads of the steps. Sometimes I wonder if this was the beginning of my PD.

There are days when my balance will be good until the afternoon; then it goes and I need to use my walker or the cane, depending on the severity of the loss of balance. If I don't use some form of support, I will fall. Some of my hardest times are when I am trying to use my walker. When the walker moves, as a result of my putting weight on it, I try to apply the brakes or move my feet, but many times I fall. My feet and brain do not react as fast as the walker moves. It is difficult. Sometimes the only way to stop is to run into something, which can be dangerous. Since the walker is fairly light, I also tend to tip it over when I try to change directions. Be careful with the walker.

I'm not sure how Parkinson's affects the body, but there are times when my body gives out. When this happens, I must stop what I am doing and get my walker or my wheelchair before I fall over. I have learned I can lay down for about an hour or so, and my body recharges itself, and in most cases my balance improves.

I was diagnosed with Parkinson's disease in 1987 and have had a taste of every kind of problem and situation. I have no idea when I am going to fall but am amazed how lucky I have been that none of the falls have resulted in serious injury. I am no longer surprised by anything that happens and am way past being depressed. I realized the reason that I fall often is because I was not being careful enough. I am rushing around too much and trying to do things too quickly. When I fall, it is almost always the same way, but so far I have never seriously hurt myself nor broke any bones. Because the falls are often it has caused me to think about broken hips. So in order to try and prevent falling I try to make myself move slower. I walk slower, I don't run and I try to plan ahead what I am going to do and how I am going to do it. My falling always happens quickly when I take chances. I just can't do anything quickly. How good my balance is on a given day will tell me if I need something to help regain my balance. I also take a bone strengthener. I think this may have helped protect me from broken bones.

One day when I was getting up from a chair, I was wobbly. It felt like there was no hip on my left side. I was standing, not hurting, but my hip seemed not to be there. I needed to make a wider turn so I would not lose my balance, since I knew if I made the shaper turn that I would go down. From my knees down I felt like my legs would not hold me up. I thought things were changing for the worse. Many hours later I realized I had forgotten to take my meds on time. In my busy day, I need to put this first, but sometimes it slips by me. When I took them I felt better.

Another problem I have is that from the inside of me I think I am humming or singing. My husband says it sounds more like a groan or moaning. I do this without thinking about it and sometimes it can get very loud. I don't know how or what is causing this problem. I know it is a flat, hoarse sound. We have talked with both my neurologist and surgeon, but they have no recommendations on how to stop it. When I realize I am making this sound, I try to stop but sometimes I just get louder.

PD came on slowly and I did not realize it at first. The first indication was that my left arm was shaking and as time went by, my left leg also started to move. One day, while walking with my neighbor, she told me that I was not walking as fast as I usually did. I also noticed I was not doing my chores as fast as usual. This stunned me. What stunned me the most was the loss of control of my legs.

Chapter Six

||||||||||||||||||||||||||||||||||||||||||||||||||||||||||||||||||||||||||||||||||||||||||||||||||||||||||||||||||

THE NEUROLOGISTS

Before I was 50, I noticed that while waiting in Church for Mass to start, or while sitting at rest, my left arm would shake. As time passed my left leg also began to shake. If my children were with me I would try to make light of the shaking by saying, "If this arm doesn't stop shaking I am going to cut it off." My husband was traveling much of the time, so I was alone. This made a difficult situation even more difficult. I was worried about myself and concerned for the children. In those day's Parkinson's disease was like a death sentence. Today, armed with the knowledge through research, people with PD have the chance to have a better life.

At the age of 46 I saw my first neurologist, who was recommended to me by my general practitioner. The neurologist wanted me to have an MRI. He said, "By having the MRI we will be able to get a better idea of what is happening to you. When you come back for your follow-up appointment we may be able to tell you what the problem is." I didn't like the MRI machine. When I was pushed into the machine I got the feeling of being very alone. When I opened my eyes there was a very bright light and the machine was very quiet and cold. It seemed like it took a very long time to do the mapping of my brain.

At my second appointment the doctor said, "Mrs. Dorsch, the whole time you were in the MRI machine your brain worked normally, but you were also shaking the entire time." I don't know what is wrong with you. He was staring at me and I was eying him back. I was thinking he was not telling me the truth. I felt he knew what was what, but wasn't telling me. I felt he was not treating me fairly. I walked out of his office feeling very let down, and I was. At that time, it was thought you had to be 60 to have PD and I was in my forties. I decided if I had to visit another neurologist it would not be him.

My arm and my leg began to bother me more and since I didn't have a good result with the first neurologist I made an appointment with my OBGyn. I had a good relationship with him, though I hadn't seen him for quite a while. I was confident that he would point me in the right direction. When I got to his office and he saw my shaking arm he didn't want to talk about anything but said "I know who you should see." He picked up the phone and made an appointment for me, a month later, with the next neurologist I was to see.

While waiting the month until the visit I was in agony: my arm would not stop shaking. When I arrived at the neurology office the waiting room was filled with patients. By the time I got to see the doctor I was not in a good mood. However, the doctor and his associate got right to work. Because there is not a definitive test for Parkinson's they began to check me with the routines that would enable them to make a determination. This consisted of trying to follow with my finger the movements the doctor was doing with his finger, touching my finger to the doctor's finger and touching my nose. Then they had me draw some circles on a piece of paper and moved my head back and forth to see how agile I was. They had me walk, checking my movements and raising my arms up and down to see how flexile I was. When they were finished they sat back, didn't say anything and sort of just stared off into the distance. I was getting irritated because of all the waiting around without knowing anything, so I said "What is wrong with me? Do you know?"

Then they said, "We think you have Parkinson's disease." They explained what it was and it scared the hell out of me. They then decided that I should take the medicine Sinemet and if my shaking stopped while on the medicine, they would know that I definitely had PD.

I saw this doctor about once a month, and all my medications stayed the same. Sinemet is one of the standard gold medications for PD, but can wear off before your next dose causing motor fluctuation called "off" episodes. After ten years the doctor commented that it appeared that my Parkinson's was arrested because I had been stable for 10 years.

The doctor I had been seeing relocated, so I had to find a new doctor and my condition began to worsen. This doctor, which I saw every month, tried to find a drug cocktail that would stabilize me, but nothing worked. A drug cocktail is a combination of drugs that would help to stabilize my PD. The doctor would say to me "you are a candidate for the new surgery." I did not understand what they were trying to tell me. When they explained the procedure, called Deep Brain Stimulation (DBS), I became motivated and finally realized that medications were not going to bring me relief. I had to do something else.

We saw two different surgeons, but rather than spending time getting to know me and my problems, they both began telling me about the operation and when it could be scheduled. We were not comfortable with them and decided to look for someone else. Duke University Hospital in Durham, NC was recommended since it was a teaching hospital. So we decided to go to Duke and get a third opinion and get a feeling about the hospital and the surgeon. The doctor suited my personality so I decided to have the operation at Duke. Later, I learned that most of the DBS surgeries performed in NC were being done at the Wake Forest Baptist Hospital just a few minutes from my home.

The neurologist arranged for me to work with a surgeon at Duke. I have stayed with this team ever since, even though they were located over 100 miles from my home. My new neurologist increased my medications which provided some additional relief. This seeking out a specialist turned out to be a good thing since the operating schedule for the DBS was delayed due to renovations being done to the facilities. The delay was several months and as the delay went on I started to experience problems that my meds weren't helping. My shaking increased, and I was losing my voice as a result of not being able to project it and I had more trouble trying to walk. It felt like my body was shutting down. I also started to dislike riding in the car, it made me very nervous, so I started to sit in the back seat. I told everyone I liked being chauffeured and taking reading material to look at on the drive. I kept calling to find out when my surgery would be scheduled and repeatedly emphasized how my condition was getting worse. They were finally able to schedule my surgery.

Our brains are wonderful. I have blocked out most of the torment I went through before the surgery. As I look back, all the neurologists along the way tried to help me and I am so grateful for their help! Since I was experiencing shaking and not sleeping at night I resorted to doing something that would make me so sleepy that I would go to sleep. My husband had just finished painting my bath. I was thinking about my children and then the idea came to me. I began to paint scenes on the walls in my bathroom using nursery rhymes. Never having painted pictures before, I was not sure how to go about it. I painted flowers from my garden and the nursery rhymes. I would repaint the scenes until I decided that was the best I could do. The first morning after I began, my mother—who was visiting me—was so surprised to find what I had done overnight. She was so complementary—most mothers are. From then on she was interested to see what I had done to the room. She would check and provide comments each morning. She could not understand how I was able to climb up two steps and not lose my balance, or how I could hold the paint brush in my hand and be able to paint when my hand was shaking so badly.

The scenes turned out to be my version of the Columbia River with a fish swimming upstream, Jack and the Beanstalk, a Camilla flower, blue spruce tree with Black Pony underneath, Humpty Dumpty, Little Miss Muffet, a cherry tree with seasonal changes and a black bird on top as well as a tropical scene from Hawaii.

Your journey will be different from mine. Your experiences will enable you, the PD patient, to begin to know yourself. Today with the improvement in the wide range of medications and surgeries, it will not seem to be a death sentence.

It is important for people to volunteer to help with "clinical trials." The process of developing new drugs is long and expensive and a drug is more likely to fail than succeed. What is a clinical trial? It is a research study involving human volunteers. These trials assess the safety and effectiveness of new ways to diagnose, prevent or treat PD. They provide insight about the disease process, and how it might be treated. Clinical trials are a vital part of research and are essential to developing better treatments.

People with PD should volunteer to take part in research projects. The lack of volunteers for research is a drawback. It is known that the lack of volunteers for research has impeded various research projects. Some research projects have died because of lack of volunteers.

When people know how critical research is to finding a cure, I hope they will volunteer.

Chapter Seven

||||||||||||||||||||||||||||||||||||||||||||||||||||||||||||||||||||||||||||||||||||||||||||||||||||||||

SURGERIES

Parkinson's disease affects millions of people worldwide with debilitating and disabling symptoms.

About 50 years ago neurologists and neurosurgeons found that making a lesion in the brain could alter the signaling paths in the neurons. This helped relieve some of the symptoms of the disease. The procedures are called Thalamotomy and Pallidotomy and destroy that part of the brain where the lesions are made. The operations cannot be reversed because the affected area of the brain is burned. These discoveries led to the latest procedure which is the placing of Deep Brain Stimulators (DBS) in the thalamus or the Globus pallida's and the fact that this operation does not kill those portions of the brain. In addition the DBS procedure is reversible.

The DBS procedure is used to treat a variety of disabling neurological symptoms such as tremors, rigidity, stiffness slowed movements and walking problems. The DBS procedure is generally used on patients whose symptoms can't be adequately controlled with medications.

I knew something had to be done! I was unsettled. My voice faded away and my shaking was uncontrollable. I asked the Blessed Mother to take care of me. I was so unsettled that I couldn't drive. Since I had tremors on both my right and left sides, my doctors and I agreed to have a bilateral implant: an implant on each side of my brain which would control my tremors and hopefully aid my walking ability.

On June 26, 2003 I had my operation. I was very tired from all the activities and the fact that I had to get up early in order to be driven to the hospital which was 100 miles away. My surgeon and the staff did a very fine job of helping to me and assure me all would be well. My surgeon told me he would stay with me until I was in the recovery room "He did."

One of my concerns was that the device called a Halo, which is secured around the head, was going to be too heavy for me to wear. I soon realized this was not the case, my concerns were unfounded.

First the surgeon performed a brain scan to locate the parts of the brain that were affecting my symptoms. Parkinson's affects the transfer of electrical signals between neurons in the brain and if these signals don't fire correctly, or misfire, the muscles either freeze up because no messages are getting through or you have tremors because the messages are coming through in rapid succession. In fact, they come in so rapidly that the affected person shakes because the muscles are expanding and contracting very rapidly.

The implants, through an electrical impulse, regulates the impulses just like a pacemaker regulates the heartbeat.

Once the mapping was completed, the electrodes were implanted into the impacted areas of my brain and wires were run under my skin from the electrodes to the back of my neck down to the batteries which were implanted in my chest and abdomen. I have two batteries, one for each electrode, but today with improvements they can make do with one battery.

At one point during the surgery, I awoke and started to move, so everything had to stop. I was not supposed to move. The next thing I remember I was in recovery with my family.

I had devoted a lot of time worrying about the procedure, mostly about the Halo that was going to be put on my head. Now I put these worries behind me, it was over. I stayed in the hospital for two days, as I was unsure of myself and the fact that we lived about 100 miles from the hospital. We wanted to be sure all was well before we went home.

Sometime after I had my implant I noticed that there was going to be a Parkinson's information meeting at one of the local hospitals.

I was so happy with the results of my surgery because I could walk without my cane, drive myself and live a near normal life. I wanted to give back, so I made plans to attend. While there, I decided to ask the doctor conducting the meeting, if he would sponsor a Parkinson's Support Group. He agreed. This was the start of the support group in Winston-Salem. For the first 10 years I went to the monthly meeting and chaired the meetings. The hospital was in charge of the agenda. Even though the agenda was professional the group was not growing. People stopped coming. There had to be a big change. There had been many improvements in PD treatments through the years. It needed to be made known and PD people needed to know they weren't alone. A drastic change was needed, so the people with PD took responsibility for the organization from the hospital. It was reorganized from top to bottom. Today the medical personal still are involved with the group but they don't make the decisions on what is done. In one year after reorganization the group has moved from 5 or 6 people to over 60 + people. With 40+ people attending monthly meetings. The group has involved a dance group with the YWCA to exercise. Their logo is "Parkinson's Forward" and it is a wonderful success story and shows what people with a serious disease can do when they have the freedom to act.

My second surgery was done on August 5, 2008 in order to replace the original batteries which had operated for five years. Several months after the replacement one of the units started to turn itself off for no apparent reason. It was a mystery to me and I was scared but it was resolved. Neither the doctors nor the Medtronic technical team could explain what was occurring, so they decided the battery should be replace and sent to the Medtronic lab for testing. So, in the fall of 2008 I had the battery, which was not operating properly, replaced. The Medtronic team never did understand why the unit did not operate properly.

Early in September of 2009 I noticed a bump developing on my head where the left electrode was implanted. A close examination by my doctor revealed that the lead was pushing itself out of position and had to be reset. This was done on September 22, 2009.

My next surgery was January 31, 2011 to replace both batteries. During this surgery I volunteered to be part of a research study to observe the response of different patterns in the electrical pulses delivered by the DBS on tremors, side effects, and bradykinesia. Duke, Winston-Salem Baptist, and Emory hospitals were involved in the study.

When I arrived at the hospital and checked in, I found two doctors who were involved in the research program looking for me. I checked my watch to see if I was late, but I wasn't. They wanted to have time with me to explain what we were going to do. I was pleasantly surprised. I was taken into the operating room and prepared for surgery. Suddenly my sinus began to drain and I was concerned about how I was going to resolve this problem. Even though I didn't need to concern myself, I still was thinking. The anesthologist gave me a long plastic tube (which I called a magic wand) to pull the mucus out of my throat. I had to laugh as I thought, "How am I going to do the testing and use the magic wand at the same time." Then my sinus stopped draining and I put the magic wand down.

The surgeon doing the battery change said if I felt anything to immediately let him know but I never felt anything. Having volunteered for the testing I was not put to sleep. One thing about PD, I forget things easily and I had forgotten that I was going to be awake for the procedure. One of the doctors who was working on the research was holding my hand and it was warm and comforting to me. Stepping forward he gave me the computer mouse which I was to use by pressing the key for the research project. As time passed I found it got harder and harder to press the key. In the meantime the operation proceeded and all was quiet in the room. At one point I started to fall asleep. I was so tired of the finger work that I could not concentrate or keep my eyes open. The doctor holding my hand held it to the end. I had to tell them to stop the testing as I was exhausted. Being awake during the testing and operation was a new experience for me. With the new batteries, I was on my way to recovery. My husband and my eldest daughter, Francesca, were waiting to take me home.

I was upbeat after my last battery replacement until I went for one of my semiannual checks in 2013, just two years after the batteries were replaced. As a result of the voltage needing to be set at a higher level in order to control my problems, the batteries were being depleted at a faster rate. They needed to be replaced, just after two years.

This last replacement was done in March of 2013 and was uneventful. However, as a result of needing to have the batteries replaced after only two years, due to the higher voltage settings, I am getting tired of having to go back for the operation so often. My doctor told me that Medtronic now have a battery that can be recharged and as a result the time between operations would be extended until such time as the battery failed or could not be recharged. The battery is also smaller than the ones I am using. The only concern I have is that I would have to make sure that I don't let the battery run down. I would have to be responsible for recharging myself. I am giving the idea of changing to the new battery serious though.

The future holds many promises for Parkinson's patients. Now when a patient needs a battery change the doctors are studying the impact of altering the rhythm and frequency of the pulses emitted by the stimulator, similar to a Morse code signal, rather than a constant beeping. They are hoping this might treat symptoms better than the current method. This new method would increase the battery life, since fewer pulse would be needed and may reduce the size of the battery and allow it to be implanted in the head rather than the chest.

Chapter Eight

||||||||||||||||||||||||||||||||||||||||||||||||||||||||||||||||||||||||||||||||||||||||||||||||||||||||||||||||||||

DISTURBANCES

There are times when I feel stupid and the things that I relate to are not available to me. I think this feeling is common to all of us. Whenever a new problem occurs I find I must draw on my experiences of the past to help me get myself going. By this, I mean I don't just float through life. I must react immediately to certain situations.

One such problem is freezing. Patients with Parkinson's disease (PD) who experience symptoms of freezing in position, being stuck while trying to walk, also have significantly impaired balance. I have not been able to work through this and it happens so quickly that it is like hitting a wall and I can't do anything but fall down. I still don't know what causes it. In the early years it didn't register with me because it was not happening to me. Then when it happened, I needed to make plans to overcome it, if I could. I needed to make changes.

Freezing is no laughing matter. Encounters with balance and freezing can be devastating. It is not being ready for the situation. It can happen in a crowd of people and it doesn't have to be many people to seem like a crowd. It can be two people and you become crowded and claustrophobia catches up with you. This is not good for a handicapped person. When seeing a handicapped person, people will naturally wait for you to go first. Everyone is watching and waiting, and it is uncomfortable for a person to be on display.

This is not good because it puts you on the spot, it highlights you. Knowing this I know I must persist. So when I begin to freeze I try hard to move out of their way as fast as I can. Sometimes it takes me a while to get myself moving. I will give a couple of examples of my freezing episodes that were very hard to take.

The YMCA was undergoing renovations to its main facilities and relocating the entrances. Several years earlier I had broken my upper left arm and even though it healed, I never recovered the full use of my arm. As a result, it was hard for me to open doors. So, I thought it would be a good idea to use the elevator and stay away from the renovations around the entrances. As I was getting ready to get off the elevator, I found that I was having a freezing moment. I could not lift my feet off the floor. I could not take a step or move. I was panicking and I was frozen in place. People were trying to help me but I could not move. Finally, after much trying, I was able to move and get off the elevator with the help of a member.

The second happening was at a party. We were walking to our dinner table when suddenly a noisy group came towards us, blocking my view. I froze and could not lift my foot off the floor. The harder I tried to lift my feet they stayed frozen to the floor. The group I was with tried to get me to move but I couldn't. When I could move they would sing and yell encouragement to me. I was embarrassed. It was a lesson to me. I needed to be better prepared for the unknown.

While all this was happening, a Good Samaritan came up to me and slipped his foot under my foot, loosening my frozen body so I was able to get to the table without trouble. There were no people near me then and that gave me the freedom to move along normally. I try to remember that in a crowd always get out ahead of everyone else or wait until I have a clear path. I still wonder about this situation and try to understand how I was able to move after my guardian angel helped me.

I still don't know what makes me freeze, and I never know what might cause it. Is it people rushing toward me? What you don't know about something can really get to you. But, whatever the reason, you must just accept it; you must just go with it because that is the way it is. Parkinson's disease does not give you chances when you are not functioning in a normal manner.

People with Parkinson's disease who experience freezing also experience disturbed rapid eye movement (REM) sleep. This study was important in that it suggests that sleep studies are able to identify rapid movement of the eyes. This study provided further evidence of a relationship between freezing and increased muscle activity during REM sleep. It is import for two additional reasons. First, it suggests that sleep studies may be able to identify which people with Parkinson's disease are more likely to experience freezing. Second, it may shed light on the biological mechanism of freezing. Freezing is a very disabling complication of PD. Unexpected happenings make PD difficult to survive. You never know what will happen next. With God's help I will hang on. I will do what He wants. The human body needs sleep just as the need for oxygen is important for survival. Sleep provides the power for the following areas to recharge: alertness, energy, mood, body weight, perception, memory, thinking, reaction time, productivity, performance, communication skills, creativity, safety, good health, long life.

Sleep disturbances are quite common, with such things as the inability to fall asleep, the inability to stay asleep, inability to turn in bed, vivid dreaming, acting out the dreams and or calling out loud, leg discomfort and pain. It is advantageous for individuals with PD to have good sleeping habits, mine aren't!

A symptom-based approach for PD patients with sleep disorders is necessary. Nocturnal behavior, excessive daytime sleeping, and insomnia are all symptoms that crop up. I have experienced them all. This constant struggle with the unknown and fear of one's symptoms is why depression is so prevalent in people with PD. I'll think my life is over—but it isn't. It's better not to dwell on the negative.

Improving sleep in PD patients, may positively affect their working memory, according to a study published recently in *Brain* (Fall 2013). Working memory is defined as the ability to temporarily store and manipulate information. It comes into play in our ability to plan, solve problems and live independently. Results showed that people with PD demonstrated better working memory, but not short-term memory, after a night's rest. Patients who were taking enhanced dopamine performed better on the test after sleeping than those who were not taking dopamine medication. The latter findings may help define the role that dopamine plays in memory. The study also showed that patients who had dementia, with Lewy Bodies (DLB), a more advanced condition of PD, showed no improvement in working memory after a night's sleep. In addition, sleep apnea, the disruption of sleep due to airway obstructions appears to impair the effects of sleep on memory.

REM sleep disorder occurs when we dream and act out our dreams. Our body turns off our muscles when we dream so we don't hurt ourselves. The muscle that doesn't turn itself off is the eye muscle. This phase of sleep is known as Rapid Eye Movement (REM). There are people who actually act out their dreams. It is important to tell your physician if this occurs. Medication may be needed. You may notice a person sleeping and you can see their eyes are moving rapidly up and down and back and forth. This is a good indication that they are in a REM sleep condition. The person is acting out their dream.

The major sleep disorders with complications for patients with PD are insomnia, behavior problems, and early morning wakening. Depression and anxiety are common with early morning wakening. People with early morning wakening may awake around 3am and can't go back to sleep.

My sleeping habits have changed. If I watch TV until 1am I find I have over stimulated myself and can't easily go to sleep, so I try to be in bed by 10:30. If I am successful I will turn on my right side and go to sleep. Another point: if I wake up, about an hour later, I find I am in a doze the rest of the night. I am not in a deep sleep. When I read that my body needs sleep to regenerate itself, it made an impression on me. I realized I need to be rested.

Another problem that I have is that my eyes want to close. This problem is known as Blepharospasm and is uncontrollable muscle movements in the eyelids. Patients with normal eyes experience involuntary closings aggravated by bright lights, wind, pollution, smoke, emotional stress and fatigue.

Another wrinkle in this weird world I live in is that when I am in bed my legs and arms will have cramps.

It is a disappointment to find the level of problems a person with a health problem such as PD has to endure. As I get older and look back, it seems unreal the length of time I have had my uninvited guest. I am frustrated that I am experiencing a smaller world because I am not as agile as I used to be.

Chapter Nine

||||||||||||||||||||||||||||||||||||||||||||||||||||||||||||||||||||||||||||||||||||||||||||||||||||||

VOLUNTEERING

After I was diagnosed with Parkinson's disease, I decided to become a volunteer for Parkinson's research when I found out that doing so might help find a cure. I went twice to Washington, DC—both times to support the Parkinson's Action Network (PAN) as they lobbied members of Congress to support an increase in funding for Parkinson's research. I wanted to be with people and learn. Being shy was part of my makeup and a problem that previously stopped me from really developing till late in life. Now l finally had the push I needed to persist.

The Journal of Health Affairs noted a medical breakthrough, but this one was not an actual drug. However, it had the same potential to alter the research and the health care landscape. I'm talking about Patient Engagement.

On face value, Patient Engagement may not sound revolutionary. Yet it represents a marked departure from traditional models of medical practice and research in which the doctor holds the knowledge and makes the decisions for us. It involves a genuinely collaborative relationship between patient and doctor. It views people not simply as patients, but as health care consumers. Engagement means inviting patients to help in deciding their treatments and including patients in determining the types of treatments, instead of letting the doctors make all the decisions.

The Parkinson's disease Foundation is extremely excited about the increased national focus on Patient Engagement. Encouraging people to take an active role in their own health care would lead to new treatments and cures.

I remember the first year I went to Washington, DC for the first Parkinson's Action Network (PAN) meeting. PAN was organized in 1991 as a nonprofit organization to serve as a unified voice advocating for better treatment and a cure for PD, as well as working with other organizations and government leaders.

We had assembled on a Saturday morning and were introduced to each other. After our first meeting, which consisted of our finding out what information we wanted to leave with Congress, we boarded the bus to go to Capitol Hill. Since this was the first year, we were concentrating on getting our congressional representatives to understand the importance of increasing funding to the National Institute of Health (NIH). At this point the NIH was not giving money to the various health care organizations for research like it does today. Senator John McCain should be noted because he helped the Parkinson's Action Network get started in the early days. The Parkinson's Action Network was set up as a political wing to provide Parkinson's disease information to members of congress. I went to the first two yearly meetings.

I was the only person from NC, so it was up to me to lobby each of the NC delegates. I often wondered if Senator Richard Burr was as nervous as I. This was his first term in office as a member of Congress. As the afternoon progressed I got to meet each representative. It was a wonderful experience. An increase in funding would allow the NIH to give more money to Parkinson's research and help other organizations also get an increase in funding.

Another way I volunteered was to talk with people who called and wanted to know the result of my DBS surgery. Would I do it again? They were trying to make up their minds concerning their own surgery. I would tell them they should run—not walk—to the nearest hospital. I told them they would be glad they did." I also volunteered to take part in tests conducted at the Duke Clinic. One of my first tests required me to use a computer mouse. They had me tap on the mouse with my index and middle finger. I would sit in a room using the computer until my meds wore off, then I would take my meds. I think I did three different tests, tapping on the computer, before my meds kicked in.

In 2011 I volunteered for a test while I was having my batteries changed. I had volunteered for the test, forgetting that I would need to be awake during the battery change. Fortunately, the doctor doing the testing was standing beside me and that gave me confidence. He held my hand and it was so wonderful. The feelings that went through me—the warmth of a human hand. The surgeon said if I felt a pin prick to let them know but I felt nothing. Next thing I remember they were readying me to leave the operating room and go home.

I also volunteered in October 2013 to reorganize a support group in Winston-Salem, now known as "Parkinson's Forward." While attending one of the PD support group meetings I noticed that there were very few people in attendance. There were only 5 people present, the moderator, the speaker, myself and two others. I mentioned to the moderator how disappointed I was that the group had gotten so small. One of the ladies said she would be willing to help revitalize the group if I would take the lead. I was getting too old to do it by myself and needed help, so since she agreed to help, I said I would take the lead. Thinking about how the group got started, I just could not let it go.

I knew what had to be done in order to bring the group back to life. I started by calling some of the early members who had PD and asked them to get involved again. I knew what positions had to be filled in order to make the group work. I started to hold weekly meetings at my home, keeping in mind that we wanted the revitalized group ready for the next monthly meeting. One day while talking to a group of friends, I mentioned that I was looking for a meeting place for the PD meeting. One of my friends said that there was a room we could use where she worked at the Red Cross.

My core group of people filled the positions needed to get started and in less than two months the group was reorganized. I can safely say that this group of people were the finest people I had ever worked with. A while later I received an email titled "AMAZING" from a member of the core group, it said:

"You are an amazing woman! Your passion to help others with this disease is incredible and you always have a smile on your face. You have every right to be angry, but you have chosen to have a great attitude and even more amazing you are trying to make a better quality life for others who suffer with PD. Never give up!"

The Michael J. Fox Foundation was established in 2000 to help find a cure for PD. The goal of the foundation is to get people with PD to volunteer to help do research that is needed to find a cure. The foundation also works at bringing people and organizations from around the world together to share information and to provide a worldwide system for people to obtain information about symptoms, trials and medications.

Team Fox was created to engage and support the people worldwide who have made it their mission to raise funds and awareness for the Michael J. Fox Foundation for Parkinson's research. The Fox Finder has initiated Community Partners to educate and show the need for clinical participation in an attempt to bring community organizers to embrace the outreach from the partners at parkinsons.org.

Chapter Ten

||||||||||||||||||||||||||||||||||||||||||||||||||||||||||||||||||||||||||||||||||||||||||||||||||||||||||||

FALLING

I was not being careful. I started to fall more and more. Eventually I had to admit to myself that this was happening because I was trying to do things—even just walking—too quickly. I've been very lucky because most of the time I fall I don't hurt myself. Every day is different, and I know based on how good my balance is in the morning if I'll need my cane or my walker that day.

Balance problems are one of the symptoms of Parkinson's disease. Balance problems increase the risk of falling, especially combined with other symptoms. In order to try and reduce falls, you must think about what you are doing and what you want to do. Do not pivot your body over your feet when making a turn, and make a wide U turn while walking. I find when I get tired, I've often pushed myself too far, which is a recipe for disaster.

One day when I was getting up from a chair I was wobbly. I thought it felt like I didn't have a hip on my left side. I was standing but not hurting. The only way I could turn was by making a wide, walking turn. Another problem is trying to open doors toward myself. When I do this I lose my balance as I pull the door towards myself and may fall backwards. Or else I will over reach and may fall into the door.

I have had problems with balance since the beginning of my PD that have caused me appreciable concern. I worried about how I might control this problem, so I started to take physical therapy to see if this might help. Therapy didn't help very much.

When I walk I feel like I am walking on egg shells. Walking is by no means easy for me. Even when I walk unencumbered it is not easy and I have to watch each step. It does not get any easier, my balance control has not improved.

I was wondering what I could do to protect my knees from getting bruised when I fell. One day, as I was watching my daughter playing soccer, I noticed the knee pads she was wearing. Since they worked for her I thought they would work for me, so I bought a pair. They worked very well and I could wear them under my dress and slacks.

I began to realize that I was falling because I was trying to keep up my old pace of living. I had to slow down. Since I slowed down I do not fall as often and I have stopped regularly wearing my knee pads. As I read more about PD and become more acquainted with the different symptoms I am better able to take care of myself.

Several factors have been shown to be associated with the history of falls: disease severity, motor impairment, postural instability, freezing of gate, leg muscle weakness, cognitive impairment, and side-effects from medication. Tell yourself when walking, "Heels down first." Heels down first is impossible for me to do. I have gotten myself into a habit of standing on the tips of my toes instead of heels down first, and I freeze.

I am amazed at the way exercises work on the body. I was not able to stand straight and I had to hold on to something in order to walk. I was very unsure about doing exercises. Suddenly, I found the exercises were building strength in my legs. I was able to walk unaided and now I am enjoying the benefit of walking with a cane or walker. I foolishly didn't want to exercise. I thought I didn't need to exercise because I had always done my own house work. I thought I was getting enough exercise that way, but I wasn't. Now I am exercising with gusto! (At times.)

I could not get around in my garden and if I got down I could not get up. I tried to push myself up, but I did not have the strength in my arms to do so. I fell on my stomach after I had been on my knees. I was not going to lay in the dirt, so I worked until I was able to get myself up. Falls, for people with PD, present a large problem. People who don't have PD do not fall as often and may not appreciate what a problem, falling can be.

Balance problems are the most frequent reasons for a fall. Freezing problems, most often, happen in confined places. One effective way to avoid falls is to take big steps and shifting your body weight. Positive self-talk, using a lighted cane, marching, and listening to music are also helpful.

Chapter Eleven

|||||||||||||||||||||||||||||||||||||||||||||||||||||||||||||||||||||||||||||||||||||||||||||||||||||||||||||||||

MY VOICE

I am perfectly fine—but I am not. This cough is so strong that I feel like I am going to choke. I need to keep my throat open. I cough more to make sure I don't choke. I find the throat area is getting to be more worry some. When my throat is dry it feels as if something is pressing down and making the opening smaller.

When I eat I must take smaller bites. Food sticks in my dry throat, making me gag. The food burns on the way down, burning like hot sauce until it reaches my stomach. There's nothing I can do to stop it and it terrifies me. When I am in public and start coughing it doesn't stop with a short cough, it will continue. My cough, I think, is very loud and draws attention. I keep cough drops with me all the time and use them to control my cough. I have trouble digesting my food and some days it will back up on me. It feels like it is in liquid form.

Most of the following information came from an article by the National Parkinson's Foundation in a booklet entitled *Parkinson's disease, Speech, and Swallowing* which can be found on their internet site, located at <u>helpline@parkinson.org</u>.

The following, from the Parkinson's Alliance, highlight some of these problems and are warning signs of a swallowing problem:

1. When eating and drinking, you choke.

2. You lose weight even though you are eating well.
3. It takes you much longer to eat than it used to.
4. You don't enjoy eating like you used to.
5. You have difficulty chewing and moving food to the back of your mouth.
6. Food sticks in your throat.
7. Your voice sounds wet during and after meals.
8. You have a history of pneumonia.

In 2001 the Parkinson's Alliance issued their first report and it covered speech difficulties PD patients may experience. About 70% of the people with PD report having problems with speech. The Lee Silverman Voice Treatment (LSVT) was recommended as a means of helping PD patients with speech problems, since slurred speech is one of the most common symptoms. I had this treatment.

Remember: If you don't use it, you will lose it.

Speech is one of the most fundamental means of connecting with others and of expressing our needs and wants. Speech difficulties can result in significant challenges when trying to interact with others and can result in functional challenges, as well as social problems which lead to a reduced quality of life.

Research has found that speech problems are common in PD and it has found that 70% of patients with PD report speech problems after the onset of PD. There is much research examining speech in PD patients and the following paragraphs are intended to provide only a brief introduction to the topic. Individuals with PD experience many problems with their speech such as monotonous, reduced pitch/volume; variable rate of speech; slurred speech; short rushes of speech, breathy, harsh sounds; difficulty enunciating words; and failing to have a rhythm of speech that reflects emotional expression.

At the start of my day I am able to talk loudly and pronounce my words distinctly, but as the day progresses I become tired and start slurring my words. My volume decreases until people are not able to hear or understand me. I am told that I am not speaking loudly and that I should face the people I am speaking to. This problem happens every day and even with repeated and frequent voice training classes it has not improved.

I find that drinking plenty of water or other liquids helps somewhat, as well as not shouting over noise and resting my voice when I am tired. I have also noticed that the amount of humidity in the air has some impact on my voice. The higher the humidity level, the easier it is for me to talk. So, I use a humidifier a lot, especially in the winter months when the air in the house is drier.

Being unable to talk with people in a normal manner is a very emotionally difficult situation and causes a lot of frustration and strain on me. It also reduces my social capabilities. It is not fair that I am not able to speak in a normal manner, but life is not fair. As time goes by I am more separated from people because I am not able to speak loud. I am using gadgets that the speech department gave me to help me breather deeper, hoping to get more air into my lungs, in order to make my voice louder. I know, my voice is gone and I will never sound sweet again but I will make myself heard.

Chapter Twelve

||||||||||||||||||||||||||||||||||||||||||||||||||||||||||||||||||||||||||||||||||||||||||||||||||||||

COPING WITH THE DIAGNOSIS

I am blowing hot and cold. So much has happened to me that am not sure what to think. As I said earlier, when something new occurs I think I've reached the end of the line. I am getting ready to fold up my tent but then I have a recovery of sorts and I feel better. This constant yo-yo is tiring and the new symptoms are not getting easier to handle. I had a setback of sorts when I went for my 6 month checkup and learned that I was using more energy in my batteries than I thought, making it necessary to have them changed in a period of 2 years. I didn't want to go through another operation so soon with my DBS/STN implants. I was not prepared for this and so it stopped me in my thinking. It caused me concern for days. I was not able to carry on my usual functions. When I had mulled over this change, I find I am now able to accept situation.

It is important to think rationally about one's health situation because you will muddy your thinking if you become emotional. We must live and we need to live with as quality a life that is possible.

The average onset of characteristic motor symptoms is initially subtle and impacts purposeful movement, occurs when people are in their sixties. People with PD also experience significant non-motor symptoms, including changes in cognition and mood, sleep disturbances, and autonomic dysfunctions. Currently available pharmacological and surgical treatments provide relief for some motor symptoms.

Bradykinesia—slowness of movement—is the second most influential factor on health status. It can affect your balance, ability to walk, and doing everyday things that are important to you. The best way to protect your motor function is to move regularly.

When I am tired my feet don't go the way I want to go. The more rested I am, the easier my legs will move.

A good exercise plan can significantly improve almost everything. Staying active remains absolutely critical. Better mobility reduces depression, treating constipation helps with mobility. Exercise regularity and taking your medications on time helps to improve your symptoms. Talk with your doctor about exercise and physical therapy.

Mobility is the ability to get around. I find this is difficult for me. I feel like I am going to topple over. You are likely going through the menu of emotions and you need to adjust yourself to the new changes you will need to make. Remember that you are not alone.

Now that you have a diagnosis you can use your freedom to learn and explore all about PD. You can begin to understand Parkinson's and its treatments. Many PD patients and their families experience knowledge in managing their disease. Patient engagement, the proactive decisions the patient makes with their doctor will help the Parkinson's patients and understand what is unknown.

Using data from over 18,000 patients, scientists have identified more than two dozen genetic risk factors involving Parkinson's disease, including six that had not been previously reported. The study reported in *Nature Genetics* was funded by the National Institute of Health and led by scientists working in NIH laboratories. Unraveling the genetic underpinnings of Parkinson's is vital to understanding the multiple-mechanism involved in this complex disease. Hopefully this will one day lead to effective therapies. Andrew Singleton, PhD and his colleagues at the NIH collected and combined data from existing wide associations studies that allowed them to find common clarinets, or subtle differences, in the genetic codes of a large group of individuals.

The investigators identified potential genetic risk variants which increase the chances that a person may develop Parkinson's disease.

My mother and her two sisters were invited to participate in the study. They were valued because they had lived so long and were in good health. They participated in the Human Genome study at Duke University. The researchers wanted to check them for gene mutations that might cause Parkinson's disease. My mother and her sisters were in their nineties at the time of the study. Today, my mother and her youngest sister, are in reasonably good health at the ages of 98 and 96. Her oldest sister died at 106.

A Parkinson's diagnosis is a life changing event that takes time to adjust to. Everyone's symptoms are different since Parkinson's is a highly individualistic disease that varies widely from person to person. I don't worry about myself and the situation I am facing. I know God is with me and he has a plan and I am constantly in contact with him. I tell him to point me in the direction he wants me to go and I will follow through.

My story was written by myself. I researched the various symptoms and I cried with all the problems I encountered. I have never been a person who cried. The crying I did was always internal until this year. All the problems I have encountered trying to use the computer, such as messing up my settings because my hand and fingers would move on their own, causing me to not know what I had done have been very difficult to contend with. I also have double vision which causes me to duplicate things over and over. It is a relief to for me to know what is happening and why and better yet, to know what to do to help myself. I am much happier now that I know what Parkinson's is. I found my faith has helped me through this horrible situation.

Chapter Thirteen

||||||||||||||||||||||||||||||||||||||||||||||||||||||||||||||||||||||||||||||||||||||||||||||||||||||||||||||

A REPRIEVE OF SORTS

Now that I have completed my efforts, I do not plan to continue studying the symptoms of Parkinson's disease and trying to remember the times I had another symptom appear.

As I said earlier, when something happened I was ready to fold up my tent, but now I have had a reprieve of sorts, if you will, since the DBS surgery. The Deep Brain Stimulation surgery, along with the new medicines and therapy, have given me hope where before there was only despair. All these treatments help me cope with my uninvited guest.

Before I had the DBS surgery I was losing ground. My balance was gone, I couldn't walk without a cane or walker, and I had to stop driving because of my shaking. After the surgery the shaking stopped but I still have to use a cane or walker to get around and I still do not drive because of my slower reflexes. I feel stronger and still try to do as much as possible, but it is hard.

I still take voice therapy in the hope it will strength my voice. The latest therapy is somewhat different than earlier ones because it dwells on my trying to strengthen my vocal cords. It is an attempt to make my throat muscles stronger so I can speak louder. This has helped me to know when I am or am not speaking loud. You can lose your voice. I did. Voice training/therapy consist of the following and may help strength your voice:

- Practice the pattern of breathing for speech.
- Strong inhalations, strong exhalations.
- Building your breath support.
- Increasing the strength and endurance of your respiratory system which is essential for loud/clear speech.
- Strengthening your laryngeal / pharyngeal muscles.
- Strengthening your vocal cords and your neck muscles.
- These are important for speech and swallowing.

Freezing causes me trouble because it keeps me from moving or walking and the more I try the worse the situation gets. As I try, I keep pushing the walker and it gets ahead of me so I fall to my knees. I need to use my walker to get around. I am finding, when I get tired, a change occurs. I am just not able to force myself to walk. I have nothing left.

When I get into bed, if I am cold, I need to get my legs and feet warm because my right foot hurts. I can't get my foot to relax so long as it is cold. I experience numbness in the first digits of my fingers and in my toes when I am laying down in bed. In order to go to sleep I must straighten my body out for the numbness to go away. I don't understand why I get this numb feeling whenever I lie down.

Recently I had taken my meds and I went to play bridge. I noticed I was not seeing the cards. I had played a heart when it should have been a diamond. Following this I played a club when it should have been a spade. I noticed that my head was moving more and more. It was about 30 minutes since I had taken my meds. This went on non-stop so I decided to stop taking my meds for 24 hours, since I felt I was over medicated.

A Parkinson's diagnosis is a life changing event that takes time to adjust to. Everyone's symptoms are different. PD is highly individualistic and varies from patient to patient.

A diagnoses of Parkinson's can become an opportunity to reexamine your priorities and focus on what you can do as a person with PD. The best recommendation that I can give is to volunteer to help in Parkinson's research. Remember that you are not alone.

My story tries to explain how I have changed and how I have stayed the same and the things that give me the most pleasure and those that give me the most hurt. When you hurt you damage yourself and any decisions you try to make. Generally, as you think through the situation, over time it will slowly fade and you can put to rest the hurt. But something needs to be put in place of the hurt.

My story was written by myself. I researched the various symptoms and I cried about all the problems I've encountered. I have never been a person who cried and the crying I did was internal, until this year. Trying to use the computer and not being able because my hands and fingers wanted to move on their own really caused me a lot of trouble because I was always messing up the computer settings or not being able to control my typing. Double vision also caused me much frustration. I am much happier now that I know what Parkinson's is and somewhat relieved to knowing what is happening and why.

I found my faith helps me through this horrible situation. You must develop a positive attitude and go forward. I don't worry as much about the situation I am facing. I know God is with me and I am relying on him to point me in the right direction and get me through. I believe that both the Apostles' Creed and the Pledge of Allegiance have helped me through tough times. One gives me faith and the other hope that our great nation will find a cure. I have included both in the hope they might help other get through their problems.

The Apostles' Creed

I believe in God, the Father Almighty, Creator of Heaven and earth;
and in Jesus Christ, His only Son Our Lord,
Who was conceived by the Holy Spirit, born of the Virgin Mary,
suffered under Pontius Pilate, was crucified, died, and was buried.
He descended into Hell; the third day He rose again from the dead;
He ascended into Heaven, and sixtieth at the right
hand of God, the Father almighty; from thence He
shall come to judge the living and the dead.

I believe in the Holy Spirit, the holy Catholic Church,
the communion of saints, the forgiveness of sins, the
resurrection of the body and life everlasting.
Amen.

The Pledge of Allegiance

I pledge allegiance to the Flag of the United States of
America, and to the Republic for which it stands, one Nation
under God, indivisible, with liberty and justice for all.

Chapter Fourteen

‖‖

PAINTINGS

Before my DBS surgery I was not sleeping at night because my arm was shaking so much that I could not relax. I knew I had to do something that would tire me out so that I might fall asleep once I went to bed. My husband had just finished painting the walls in our bathroom and the idea came to me to paint pictures on the walls. Never having painted before, I was beyond understanding what I was getting into: I just plunged into the task hoping that my arm would stop shaking for at least a short period of time. I decided to paint nursery rhymes and things that were important to me.

The first situation I used was to remember my granddaughter, Amelia Katherine. We had her for 6 months as she was a Down's Syndrome baby.I drew Humpty Dumpty sitting on the wall. I placed the first drawing in the corner of the bath behind the door so if we kept the door opened he would not be seen.

When my mother got up the next morning she was so surprised to find what I had done during the night. After this she was encouraging, every day as she would come to see what I had done overnight.

I was beyond understanding. I had craft paint left over from one of the craft stores and so I used it. My next picture was of two blue birds the husband was high up in a Red Heart Tree looking down to see what the other bird was doing.

The next scene was when we were in Oregon we drove by the Columbia River the fish were trying to swim upstream. My youngest daughter was with us. She would not get up from lying on the back seat to look at the river. She was listening to her music. Along with this scene I painted the Jack and the Bean Stalk story.

Because I had spent so many years traveling to Hawaii I painted the next scene: one of tropical plants and a beautiful water fountain. I don't recall planning to paint this...it just appeared. I remember one day I locked myself out of my hotel room. I went to the desk and told them my story. The clerk gave me money to get lunch.

I abstracted a magnolia tree we had planted in the front yard. The next scene was a large cherry tree. I painted it pink and the second part of the tree was green. At the top of the tree was placed a black bird for our son. At the bottom of the tree was painted various flowers from my garden.

The final scene I painted was of Little Miss Muffet. I used to sing this rhyme to my oldest daughter as she sat on her tuffet.

The following photographs are of some of the wall paintings, and I hope they demonstrate what you can do even if you have PD.

HUMPTY DUMPTY

Our first granddaughter, Amelia Katherine, inspired this painting.
We only had her for six months. She was a Down's
Syndrome baby with severe health complications. I used
the Humpty Dumpty rhyme to depict her problems.

RED HEART TREE

My husband had planted several seedling in our
back yard which grew into nice trees.
The tree, with two blue birds, one watching the other, was my
attempt of depicting my husband always looking out for me.

COLUMBIA RIVER & JACK IN THE BEANSTALK

On a trip to Oregon with our young daughter we visited the Columbia River and saw the salmon swimming up- stream. I was very impressed and wanted her to remember that exploring the unknown is important so I used the Jack in the Beanstalk story.

BLUE SPRUCE TREE

We had received several Blue Spruce seedling from my Dad,
who lived in Pennsylvania. We brought them to North Carolina
and planted them in our yard. I was amazed that they grew
so well, due to the fact that the climate was so different.

HAWAII

We had gone to Hawaii several times, so I decided that I should include a version of Hawaii into my art work. I don't remember painting the water fountain; it was just there when I was done.

GREEN & PINK CHERRY TREE

We had many cherry trees in our yard, thanks to the birds and mother- nature. My abstract, green and pink, attempts to show the tree in full bloom and when not in bloom. The black bird represents our son and a company, Blackbird that he started.

LITTLE MISS MUFFET

Our eldest daughter had beautiful blond hair as a child and I would sing the Miss Moffat nursery rhyme to her at bed time. This is she, sitting on her tuffet. She did not like me singing about her.

BLACK PONY

A favorite story my mother use to tell me and my brothers and sister, and later on to my young children, was that of the Sandman coming with his Black Pony and his bag of sand to put children to sleep at bed time. My black pony has an extended back, in order that several children could ride on him to sleepy time.

FLOWERS

My husband liked to grow large flowers so I
included some of these from our garden.

FLOWERS

Another version of the many flowers, along with
the many bees that were always visiting.

Resources

Booklets from the National Parkinson's Foundation

      Mind, Mood and Memory
      Caring and Coping
      Practical Pointers for Parkinson's Speech and
          Swallowing, 2nd Edition
      What You and Your Family Should Know, 3rd Edition
      Medications, 4th Edition
      Nutrition Matters
      Fitness Counts

Parkinson's Outcomes Report to the Community. The National Parkinson's Foundation. 2009.

The First Report DBS/STN Patient Survey, Parkinson Alliance. 2003.

Parkinson's Alliance Survey, Non-Motor Symptoms PD. 2012.

DBS4PD.org, Falls and Fear of Falling. 2013.

DBS4PD.org, Sleep in Parkinson's Disease. 2014.

DBS4PD.org, Autonomic Systems in PD. 2014.

PCORI study on the prevention of falls in older adults.

Michael J. Fox Foundation Website

Motor and Non-Motor Symptoms, Parkinson Disease Foundation Website

Eat Well, Stay Well with Parkinson's Disease by Kathrynne Holden, MS.RD. 1998.

Medtronic Corporation Website